The Book of Evil

The Book of Evil

poems by

Jason Bredle

Dream Horse Press
California

Dream Horse Press
www.dreamhorsepress.com
Editor: J.P. Dancing Bear

Dream Horse Press
Post Office Box 2080
Aptos, California 95001-2080
U.S.A.

Bredle, Jason
        The Book of Evil
                p.40

                        ISBN 978-1-935716-09-9
                        1. Poetry

10 9 8 7 6 5 4 3 2 1

First Edition

Cover: "Abstract 421" by Nataera.
http://www.nataera.fr/index.htm

Contents

The Book of Evil

for Rebecca

The Party

Salt Lake City, 1999, I wake on a bed of landscaping. Across the pool, I see my boo grinding with another man. I hope nobody's drawn a dick on my face. There are so many vibrant colors. More importantly, music can never be loud enough. It's as if I've never seen my hands before this moment. Ja Rule is on fire. It's impossible to bench press too much. What happened to my shirt? It looks like I spilled a cabbage salad, a glass of fruit punch and all of today's gelato flavors all over it. Please don't make me go in the sun. Do I have all my organs? I just want to find my shoes and space out for a while. President Jimmy Carter defines a party as a social gathering intended for pleasure or amusement. This party is off the hook.

Suburban Love Song

Suddenly you realize you're in the middle of it and it's heartbreaking. You receive a telephone call from yourself in the future telling you to run. All I want to know is if you're mad at me. If I could, I'd tattoo your name on my skeleton. I love to look outside. I love to be outside. I love when you touch the back of my head. I love when you hold me in your arms. I hope summer never ends. It's twilight. I hear children playing. I hear sprinklers, a lawn mower. Airplanes descend over the backyard onto the nearby runway. This is where we live. Hell at its most tranquil. To flee is life. To linger is death. The only thing wrong with this picture is everything. It's the eve of a hostage situation. Will you do one thing for me tonight? Will you put on your favorite dress and sit with me?

The Proselytizer

Emotionally speaking, I'm a mess. Have you ever read what's his name? Space and time are a fabric that surrounds us. Tell me what you know about the velocity of the universe. One night, I thought really, really, really hard until an omnipresent male voice spoke to me. He told me I could be king if I perform a few tasks. I had to transcribe everything he said, I had to tell you what he told me, and I had to circumcise myself. It felt like the end of the beginning. Thirty years later, here I am. The same goes for music. It's all inspired by a true story. It started with a fist of white light. It exploded. Knife in one language means wound in another. There's no cosmological constant. Just look at the night sky. We're someone else's heaven.

Platypus Boy

It was one of those things: a mad scientist, crazy guy, world leader and a costumed vigilante gathering to discuss the fate of the planet. I liked the vigilante because he could be anyone and had a really cool outfit. I wouldn't want to have one hole for everything. My teacher continues to appear in my dreams. She's hot. I don't like the taste of oxygen. Lactating without a nipple sounds hard. One solution is to turn all air into water. I always begin by interrogating myself: where was I on the night of June 12? In some villages carnal knowledge is an assumption. You pick berries in the woods with your daughter until she vanishes. There's too much music. Some of the greatest super heroes have been monotremes. Ever hear of Platypus Boy?

The Wetlands

Every time I devise a plan I realize it's going to fail the moment I enact it. I think I'm in love with you but I don't think you're in love with me. I like walking with you across the footbridge. Do we hold hands? Around us we hear the noise of insects and birds I wish I knew the names of. Is the sun low in the sky? Tell me the angle of our shadows. I feel sad but it's the sad you feel when you realize the world itself is intrinsically sad and you want to drink tea with it while holding a neighbor's cat hostage in a small mountain home heated by a stove. Do I sound crazy? Can you believe I used to hate the wetlands? I thought they were boring. My plan had always been to get as far away from them as possible. It was even my quote in my high school yearbook: "My plan is to get as far away from the wetlands as possible. Stay sweet, don't ever change." What will become of us? There's a gazebo here. We huddle inside it until you pee into my hand. It's warm. I don't really know what happens after this. Do I already feel loss? It is the end of one life, it's the beginning of another.

The Contestant

Dunking your screaming head into a tank of scorpions, removing your screaming head from a tank of scorpions and dunking your screaming head into another tank of scorpions is something you do for someone you love. Have you ever tasted cat excrement? Have you ever gathered around a bonfire with gorgeous people on a tropical island and cried as you watched a video of someone you love flirting with someone you hate? Some might say even if you lose you'll still get a year's supply of hygiene products. That's not enough. What does the survey say? I want the Hyundai with California emissions. I want a new living room. I want an electric guitar and I want Jim J. Bullock, Shadoe Stevens and Alf to help me win it. Pass me that plate of one thousand hot dogs and five liters of mustard. If I think of death as a blessing, no one will defeat me. I need immunity from the next elimination. I'm going to win this challenge. That's my final answer.

City of Lavender

I had everything I ever wanted to say to you organized in my head but forgot it all when you took my palm in your hand and with your index finger wrote "disaster." If you were to ask me how I ended up here, I don't even know. Every night at 8:25 I can't believe it's already 8:25 and I'm so happy it's only 8:25. Sometimes I find tragedy reassuring. Sometimes the cat licks my neck. I don't want to think about where I've been or where I'm going anymore. Sometimes I just want to cry. Sometimes I just want to sit in a quiet space. It's within me to rip my own head off. Let me tell you about the city. It's a city of lavender. I can't remember its name. There aren't enough bank holidays. Someday you'll read this and understand what type of person I am.

Pep Talk

It starts with the Santa Ana winds. High-pitched noises begin to annoy you. Are you ready for me to say something controversial? Getting man and wolf to mate isn't easy, but it's your assignment. Today I found a stuffed animal that looks exactly like the neighbor's cat. I hate myself for not buying it. Things like this usually happen in more sinister provinces. The villagers know something you don't. Should you follow that dwarf? Wait, wait, you're not putting me in this oubliette, are you? I like Coke more than Pepsi. I've been shaving so much lately. This is what happens when you start a revolution of smiles and feet. You're crushed by the empire. Your friend is dead, a moon branded on his chest. You insist on driving with your head out the window. It begins to mizzle. Even though it's making you crazy, you're totally going to beat this werewolf thing.

The Champion

Put me in a room with anything and I'll win. This includes chimps. If the room is empty I'll be more empty. A square of sunlight rises west and sets east of my heart. I have to drink so much Orangina by 11:30. The neighbor's cat likes to nap in the sunlight square. He's the solution to most of my issues. I'm trying to be somebody. Have you heard the new music? You could probably snap my shins in half right now. There are a lot of white towels covered with blood. I'm prepared to hold a revolver to the cat's head, hold the cat to the window and yell "I'll freaking do it, man!" at any moment. There are a million things I have to tell you. When my heart darkens, I lie in a corner and the cat crawls into my arms. I have to make a choice between good and evil. I'm the most talented raw superstar there is.

Splash Country

Some prefer an inner tube and water wings. Others prefer iced tea and nectarines. It's pretty simple: waterslides are insane when you have a beard but you go faster without one. Have you ever watched the sun rise over the wave pool? Tell me what you think of our newest attraction. This room is roomy with a capital r. To wit: there's too much to read. Have you ever made love on a lazy river? Sometimes I like to drive with binoculars. If I ever have a son, I'll tell him this: you only have one chance to be young. I'm the Director of Leisure. I let everyone sunbathe topless. My jai alai and mixed doubles tournaments are legendary. I can teach you how to surf. You'll spend your nights waiting for the next day. You'll spend your days waiting for the night. You, my friend, are going to get wet. Welcome to Splash Country.

Family Feud

Quilting a flower is easy. When beating someone with a musical instrument, never underestimate the piccolo. It'll surprise you. I used to have imaginary conversations all night long with women I loved. The next morning was depressing. It's the typical story. What begins as a fun family outing quickly dovetails into bitter resentment and anger. Who takes onions and Grand Marnier to the beach? Sometimes I call the neighbor's cat Christophe, international cat of mystery. I think he likes it. We happened upon a restaurant that serves the best bowl of goo. They say at the moment of death to carry everyone's suffering. I've seen a man shoot a cat in the head with a revolver. Are we watching a fight scene, an abusive relationship or a home movie? Richard Dawson sort of creeps me out. Will you wrap this medicine in bread? They say after death our experience will be choiceless. I would've written this sooner but last month I broke all my fingers and thumbs in a wide receiving accident.

The Paranoid Ambersons

The Paranoid Ambersons is an interesting concept but I don't know anything about the family. It could be Father is crouching in the crawl space or it could be he's in his workshop making a rocking horse. What was that rustling? It could be the house settling or it could be a ghost. What was that? Did you hear that? I hear someone speaking Polish. Wait, that's English. No, it's Polish. For the love of freak, Mother, please walk softly. If I ever become a ghost I'm going to haunt the family living in the house where I was killed. Is it deceptive for a realtor not to tell families about a possible haunting in a home? It's not that difficult to be honest. Everyone on the block knows. I grew up in a haunted house and it's frightening. I'll never play ping-pong again. Shhh! Stop talking so loudly. It's too loud. There's too much noise. It's just so much. I mean it's a lot. It could be Dad's working on his rocking horse or there could be some type of super scary evil spirit. No, I'm serious. Everyone on the block knows. This is too loud.

The Pyramid

Whenever I see a rising drawbridge I consider jumping it. Everywhere I go I like to pretend I'm being chased. Once I shared a limousine with an interpreter at the Nuremberg trials. It feels like it's going to thunderstorm. It's not easy to take a cat on a boat. One of my earliest memories is of a dream. I was near a pyramid in the jungle. I couldn't find you and my teeth were falling out. It was as if I knew people but I didn't know people. I'm a quadruple threat. I open my memory book and bring memories to life. Once upon a time there was a cat. One thing led to another and the cat became my hostage. Yet he took me so many places I couldn't have reached by myself. I like to think the pyramid had something to do with this. There have been many great pyramids throughout history. If you were to stack those pyramids on top of one another to create one big pyramid, this pyramid would be at the top of that pyramid.

The Club

I read something upsetting in a magazine. One summer I ate a spoonful of salt and butter every morning at 10:00. The sports team I supported was suspended on allegations of cheating. My father was miserable but acted as if he wasn't. We'd climb the fence, play tennis and swim in the country club pool after dark. It turned out he was doing cocaine but I didn't know it. In retrospect, it was the 90's and the guy was still playing with a wooden racket. There are many clubs you could join. In some you're spanked and in others you're brainwashed. I'm going to be so late because I have to stop at a bookstore and buy a gigantic coffee table book of old maps. In Spanish they call a club sandwich a "club sandwich." I wrote this, lost it, then rewrote it from the memory of having written it. What do you think so far?

The Promise

If you're ever passing through the countryside and an old lady with grotesque features stops you and tells you to beware, you're entering a place of pure evil and it's best to turn back now before it's too late, just turn back. Why fight it? If her features are normal, it's your decision. If she has one or two grotesque features but otherwise she's normal, you're thinking too much. I'm really becoming attached to the cat. We're at the lake house. No one will look for us here. We spend most of our time reading, sleeping and eating sparrows. There's an IGA in town. I set up an account at a nearby video store under a false name. They have a surprising amount of pornography. In the morning, the cat gets under the covers with me. We doze to the sound of waves lapping the shore outside the bedroom. Do you like a cool breeze? I've painted a hex on the front door. I think if you hold something hostage long enough it becomes yours. In the middle of the night you ask if there's music. There is no music. Promise me that someday you'll listen to what I'm trying to tell you.

Spontaneous Overflow of Emotion Recollected In The Sea of Tranquility

Lately my dreams have been haunted by penises. Never before have I stood on the shores of so many seas and felt so empty. I miss your hair. How are the cherry blossoms? Describe to me the spring rain. I'm sad my cricket died. I've replaced him with a basketball I named Spalding after Spalding Gray. I saw something like this in a movie once and it seemed like a good idea. As you may imagine, Spalding and I have many, many lively discussions on a variety of interesting topics well into the night. Masturbating in one sixth the gravity of earth is fun. It feels crazy when I ejaculate. I miss your cooking. I want a Dr. Pepper. I want to play catch with a child. When I close my eyes all I see are butterflies. When I close my eyes all I see are strawberries. That shaking my hands do? It's getting worse. If I tell you something, will you swear not to tell anyone? Love is a wet helmet. I can feel it. I'm on the verge of a psychological breakthrough.

Bathtub of The Humble Administrator

I have such zany friends. There's the Chinese guy who's always in the bathroom, the guy who won't let you out of the stairwell if you've accidentally locked yourself inside because somebody told you the elevator was broken, the woman who yells at you for trying to organize a Halloween party and the other Chinese guy who's always in the bathroom. Did you ever find the diner that serves those delicious nighthawks? Here's something I've never told anyone. There are tiny dolphins in my bathtub. Sometimes I feed them tiny fish. After tiny fishermen showed up to catch tiny tuna, the tiny dolphins began to disappear. That was when tiny Greenpeace arrived. There's no glory unless you put yourself on the line, and even then there's not a lot of glory. You have many different tiny fish in a bathtub and you have many different tiny people fighting over the fish. And then you have the tiny dolphin, which isn't a tiny fish, but a tiny mammal. What I don't understand is who's in the market for all these tiny tuna.

The Book of Evil

There's a guy out there who likes to dangle his genitals in his aquarium. I like butterscotch pudding. It's true I've dibble dabbled in the occult philosophies. Here's a mantra: go out, go wild and do it again and again. Out there conversations about model rocketry dissolve into the night. You talk until you question how you ever got into this conversation about what kind of job you can do with no hands. I have some personal issues I really need to deal with at the moment. When there's music I make up little dances to do with the neighbor's cat. He tolerates them. Did a disembodied voice just insult my maturity? I think we're in trouble because the cat spends more and more time pacing and looking at me as if waiting for me to do something. I'm on the couch bombarding myself with incredible scents. I wish I could drink from the fountain of forgetfulness. We're running out of places to hide. We'll have to leave for another place soon. I don't want to go to that place because there's a book of evil buried there.

The Glacier

Arms are a weird body part to hate. Everywhere I'm looking at rainbows. How do you say "quicksand" in your language? Do you find my jackets irritating? What about the number of times I change them? I too once knew someone with many irritating jackets. When I pick up hitchhikers they ask what church I attend. Sometimes the music can be so much like ice. The same thing happened to Paolo. He went through the looking glass. Education is a ray of light. I'm taking the neighbor's cat west! I want to, you know, live inside a sunset. I never knew a place could be so beautiful. I love your arms. Have you ever put your tongue on a glacier? You can change my sentences. I'll accede to a demand. Please, teach me how I should do it.

Jofer Ranch

One thing I miss is the spectacle of 7:30. I like riding in the taxi with you because of the way your bare arm brushes against my bare arm. Do you feel the same about me? Tell me what you think of the bananas and cream. Here's something controversial: I pose for a photograph in front of a statue of a horse with a huge erection. Is innocence only a product of my imagination? I've learned that a certain combination of sunlight and wind will cause a person to fall asleep driving. When I wake terrified in the middle of the night, you touch the back of my neck and it goes away. The mere presence of a swimming pool amazes me. It's one of those days you want to take a neighbor's cat under your arm and climb to the top of a mountain shaped like Jesus. For once I feel as if I have no burdens. What I fail to realize is that you do. Someday you'll throw away all your photographs and forget me. Red next to yellow and you're fucked. Few people have the magic to make everything they say coherently.

Zion

Here's an important question: what is it, overall, that you're kind of looking for? The neighbor's cat and I are on the run, driving cross country, each of us with our respective heads out our respective windows. It's typical we don't have time to think about anything we do before or while we do it. Behind every beautiful place is a massacre. I wish I knew what's going on inside his head. One thing to do is cover all the drains, run hot water and leave. This isn't how I'd imagined it. The sunlight is nice but I always have a headache. Sometimes we pull onto the side of the road, open the cooler and have ice cream. I like to feel the cat's warm body against my cheek. Everywhere you go you wonder what they know. Eventually someone will retrace your steps. Someone will try to understand what you were going through. You're the dawn star. You write a letter to your family. You fold the letter into an infant's shoe. You leave the shoe in a field of wildflowers. I've seen the cat chase and eat a dragonfly. I don't want to live. I wish I were dead. I've said the words so many times they don't mean anything anymore.

Acknowledgments

Another Chicago Magazine, "Platypus Boy," "Pep Talk," "The Pyramid"

The Collagist, "The Proselytizer"

DIAGRAM, "Spontaneous Overflow of Emotion Recollected in the Sea of Tranquility," "The Club," "The Book of Evil"

The National Poetry Review, "City of Lavender"

The Nepotist, "Jofer Ranch"

Requited, "Suburban Love Song," "The Wetlands," "Family Feud"

Saltgrass, "The Champion," "The Promise," "Zion"

Thanks to my family, friends and cats.

About the Author

Jason Bredle is the author of *Smiles of the Unstoppable, Pain Fantasy, and Standing in Line for the Beast,* as well as the chapbooks *Class Project* and *A Twelve Step Guide.* He lives in Chicago.

Previous winners of the Dream Horse Press National Poetry Chapbook Prize:

2008—*Thirteen Curses (and other love poems)* by T.J. Beitlemen
2007—*Incorporated* by Charles Sweetman
2006—*The Small Anything City,* by Cynthia Arrieu-King
2005—*A Unified Theory of Light,* by Theodore Worozbyt
2004—*Wait for Me, I'm Gone,* by Amy Holman
2003—*Adam & Eve Go to the Zoo,* by Jason Gray
2002—*New Fables, Old Songs,* by Rob Carney
2001—*The Florida Letters,* by Ryan G. Van Cleave